PARENTING

A COMPLETE GUIDE

PARUL RAMANI

Parul Ramani
1st Edition

Publication Date: September 2022
Price: ₹ 499 $ 6.26
ISBN: *978-93-95673-42-6*
Published by:
Adhyyan Books
Office No. 125,
Opposite Vivanta by Taj,
DDA SFS. Pocket-1, Dwarka,
Sec-22, New Delhi-110077
Website: http://adhyyanbooks.com
E-mail: contact@adhyyanbooks.com

Printed at: Repro Printers, Delhi

CONTENTS

TO MY DEAR PARENTS,

Parenting itself is the learning process throughout the journey. It is the most fulfilling job that we will ever have, but it's not without any challenges. Modern family life is stressful and with various pressures on families, parenting is not always easy. Ultimately parents want what is best for their child and a strong parent-child relationship can help lead to better outcomes for children.

Most often parents know well that how their parents had raised them and based on their on childhood experiences, they add on or reshape their method of nurturing. Traditional parenting has a lot more restrictions and boundaries over their children. However traditional parents focus is to raise responsible and functional adults with good manners, proper education and worth ethic. While the modern parenting is so much flexible. The focus is nurture, involvement and allowing children to express themselves individually and freely. Here I am trying to put some ideas which are already implemented by lakhs of parents with my own experience also as a parent. Though parenting is a challenging task, with implementation of some proper method we can raise our child as an independent, successful, good human being with all good values.

Learning starts from birth, not just when a child enters preschool. It's important to give a child, space to try things on their own and make mistakes. This is when they'll form their independence and figure out how the world works for themselves. It's a part of their journey of learning. Child development refers to a physical, linguistic, cognitive and emotional changes that occur in a child from the time he/she is born to early adulthood. All of these dimensions are interdependent and include:

- Social and emotional growth
- Language and communication
- Movements and physical development
- Cognitive growth (learning, thinking and problem solving)

All these aspects are crucial for healthy development and growth.

Remember you are the only person as a parent who can understand your child better than anyone else. Try to understand them. Love them unconditionally.

First step is to form a connection with your child and built a strong parent-child relationship. It is playing an imperative role in the holistic development of child. Your bonding helps to shape up desire personality of your child. Also minimize the risks of undesirable behavior. Ultimately we all wish to be the best parent for our children.

In this book I have tried to cover all the key aspects of parenting as well as how to give proper direction to your child, how to incorporate discipline to them. I have tried to give answers of all of your questions like fostering values and achieving success in academic and in practical life, as well as importance of your bonding to your child. By reading this book, you will be able to easily recognize your child's personality too. If you want to discover the genius self of your child than this book is made for you. Thank you for reading my book.

1

BE A ROLE MODEL

"Your child will follow your example, not your advice."

As a parent you are the role model of your child. Parents want their children to excel in whatever they do. The best way is to start with you. You can inspire your child by becoming a role model. Children learn the most from their parents, if you act as a role model for your child, it may help in shaping your child in a positive way

- Your child is spending most of his/her time with you and thus learns a great deal from you. They are greatly inspired by you.
- Your choices of friends help in determining what kind of people your child will be friendly with.
- Your day-to-day core and lifestyle choice influences your child's choice too.
- Your relationship with your life partner and relatives also helps in shaping up how your child would perceive his/her relationships.
- Your attitude towards academics, sports and other aspects of life impact your child's choice too.

- Your child just needs your unconditional love, care and guidance to be successful in his/her endeavors.
- The first five years of child are very crucial to sow the seeds of learning.

This is the time when the foundations for learning, health and behavior throughout life are laid down.

In the first five years of life, experiences and relationships stimulate children's development, creating millions of connections in their brains.

In fact, children's brains develop connections faster in the first five years, than at any other *time in their lives.*

Children's brain is like a sponge, it soaks up huge amounts of vocabulary, information and skills, creating millions of neural networks in their brains.

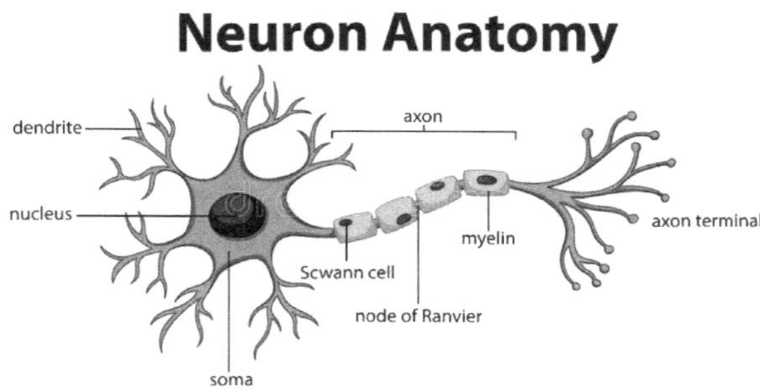

Developmental milestones act as a practical guideline of ideal child development.

Social scientists have shown that much of learning that occur during childhood is acquired through observation and imitation.

For most of the children, the most important role models are their parents and caregivers, who have a regular presence in their lives.

Role modeling is one of the most powerful tools, you have in your parenting tool belt to influence the direction of your children's character, whatever their age might be. When used to best advantage, you can pass on the values you want your child to adopt so that they become the adults you would like them to be.

Through role modeling, you have the ability to influence your children's development in positive ways and make it more likely that they become people you will admire when they become mature.

▸ So, make a checklist to review your own behavior and attitudes.

How do you:

- Handle stress and frustration
- Express anger
- Tackle the problems
- Behave/treat other people
- Show the gratitude
- Celebrate the occasions
- Spend the time with family
- Speak
- Show your emotions
- Deal with responsibilities
- Deal with competition

• Deal with any loss or mistakes

• Handle any adverse situations

• Behave with your spouse

• What do you eat

• How much do you exercise

• You can add as many points as you want in your child.

‣ Your children are not only watching you carefully for clues about how to be; they are also listening to you . the way you speak, what you speak about and the opinion you express will influence their values.

- Do your words show respect for others?
- How is your voice tone. Whether is loud, harsh or mild?
- Children value your words and your tone too. Do not yell or shout at a child when insisting on a point.
- You can express great deal from your tone. Do not make it hurtful

In short, be the best version of yourself.

Whatever values you implement in your life.

If you haven't thought of becoming a role model for your child, start now. Ultimately parenting is to be ready to learn at every moment and implementation process for giving true values to your child. If you want them to have integrity, compassion and civic-mindedness, tell the truth, work hard, keep their temper and value family, then that's exactly what you need to do yourself.

Values you want in your child.

(child-name) ________________

Make a list

MORAL OF THE CHAPTER:

✓ For children, parents should be their role models, since children always imitate the actions of the people around them, which mean that it is important to be a virtuous parent and give your child a good example.

✓ There is no school equal to a decent home and no teacher equal to a virtuous parents.

✓ Make a list of values you want in your child and fill the given chart.

2

HOW TO BOOST YOUR CHILD'S SELF-ESTEEM

"Parents need to fill a child's bucket of self-esteem so high that the rest of the world can't poke enough holes to drain it dry."

Children develop their self-esteem from how they are treated as a child. If they receive proper love, care, protection and validation, they will definitely develop good self-esteem.

As a parent, when you give your unconditional love and support to your child, they feel good about themselves. One of the great secrets of being positive and self-confident is feeling good about yourself. Make them feel good. Assure them that as a parent, you are there to support your child always. Make them feel protected. Allow them to do things according to their interest..

- **Never underestimate your child.**

Never judge your child on the basis of his or her marks or grade in the school. Someone who is not interested in studies can be interested in something else which he/she can master.

The most important part about the child who is not up to the mark in school is that they follow their dreams. In fact, a number of successful people did poorly in school. Steve Jobs, for instance, he never completed his college, yet he became a successful and world-famous inventor and entrepreneur.

Intelligence cannot be defined by grades or exams, and exam results do not determine success in life. But the most important thing to follow their dreams and prove themselves is your abundance support and belief in them. It is your strong belief in them, that is able to grow their self-esteem.

Let me explain with one more example that how can you as a parent influence your child and raise their confidence.

A great example, how Thomas Alva Edison's mother was the making of him.

Thomas Alva Edison

One day, a young Thomas Edison came home from school and gave a letter to his mother. He told her, "My teacher gave this to me and told me to only give it to my mother." As his mother began to read the letter her eyes began to swell with tears. Overcome with emotions she read the letter to a young Thomas: "Your son is a genius. This school is not advanced enough and doesn't have enough good teachers to teach him. Please teach him yourself." Thomas, after hearing these words grew with excitement and expectation, and those words motivated and inspired him.

Many years later his mother passed away. At his mother's home, packing away her belongings, he stumbled upon the folded letter written by his teacher. He read the letter but this time its contents did not sound like what he heard when he was young. The letter stated: "Your son is mentally ill. He can no longer attend our school. He is expelled." His mother did a great job by keeping the negative from his ears and replacing it with what was possible for him.

Edison became one of the greatest inventors of all time because he became the words he heard the first time. What would've happened, and what would we lack today, if Thomas heard the true context of the letter? His mother's boldness to replace the words was right to prepare him for destiny.

The impact, a parent made on a pioneer, whose break through made a world changing impact.

- **More encouragement, less criticism**

Avoid making loaded statements or using words as weapons. Comments like " What a stupid thing to do!" or "You act more like a baby", this causes mental damage just like physical harm.

A fascinating article published in The Journal of Clinical Child and Adolescent Psychology found that children who are constantly being criticized develop a habit of avoiding looking at other people's facial expressions—whether those people are expressing positive or negative feelings. By avoiding looking at other people, children's ability to receive positive information and make positive social connections with others is undermined. Researchers suggest that this could lead to anxiety and depression in that child.

More and more scientific research shows how parenting and education techniques around encouragement rather than criticism can lead to a healthier self-image and positive behavior in your children. With depression, anxiety, and suicide on the rise for youth across our nation, it is more important than ever to examine how we parent and talk to our children during these early childhood years.

Praising accomplishments will make them feel proud, letting kids do things independently will make them feel capable, strong and will boost their confidence.

Allow kids to fail.

Let your kids know that everyone makes mistakes, that you still love them a lot, even when you don't love their behavior.

It's natural to want to protect your child from failure, but trial and error is how kids learn, and falling short on a goal helps kids find out that it's not fatal. It can also spur kids to greater effort, which will serve them well as adults

Here I want to give an example of a famous personality who faced many failures.

Isaac Newton:

Isaac Newton was an English mathematician, physicist, astronomer, theologian, and one of the widely recognized scientists in the scientific revolution. Newton gave the world, the new form of the earth with laws of motion and universal gravitation.

Isaac had a hard childhood with a stepfather he hated so he lived with his maternal grandmother. Isaac went to school to learn Greek and Latin which probably imparted a foundation of mathematics. He was removed several times from the school and his mother attempted to make him farmer, the occupation he hated the most.

But his love for mathematics was persistent and made him one of the greatest scientists of the time.

Isaac Newton

Always be ready to give next chance to your child.

I have one simple question to all parents, that when your child first time learns to start walking, many times they fell down and how many times you encourage them to start learning once again to walk?

If you can show your complete belief at that time, why can't it be every time?

When you can give chance to learn a simple walk for many times and up to many days. You can also give chance to them for other tasks like grades for academics or start a new business.

Be there as a backbone.

Your one little sentence is more than 1000 other inspirations. Just say you can do it.

They definitely will do it.

There are a lot of inspirational stories of famous personalities, who became what they are today because of their mother's teachings.

The famous Indian personalities like Mohandas Karamchand Gandhi, Abdul Kalam, Narendra Damodardas Modi, Shahrukh Khan, and Sachin Tendulkar are greatly influenced by their parents only.

Here I want to share a **brief story about how Narendra Modiji is influenced by his mother.**

Narendra Damodardas Modi

Known better as Narendra Modiji- this man is currently running our nation as the Prime Minister of India. Modiji was a tea-seller back in his early days and later moved ahead to where he is today. This sixty-nine-year-old man treats the nation as his mother. Though the mother of our PM does not live with him, and the reason she gives is- What will she do with him? What will they talk about? Also, Modiji clarifies in one of his interviews that his mother hates it when he returns late at home (after all, a mother is always a mother).

Encourage your children to discover what he or she is passionate about. It may take a few tries along the way. Support your child on the journey toward passion and urge him or her to keep going until he or she finds out what it is.

- **Motivate kids.**

Maintain a positive and optimistic outlook for your children. If they see fear or doubt in your eyes, they likely will lose self-confidence. Having a positive approach will brighten their outlook on a situation.

Pay attention to what your child does well and enjoys. Focus more on strengths than weaknesses if you want to help kids feel good about them.

Learn about your child's interests. Talk to your child about them and listen. It will show your children that you care and that they are free to talk to you about their interests.

Show your love.

Let your child know you love him no matter what. Win or lose the big game, good grades or bad. Even when you're mad at him. Making sure your child knows that you think they're great — and not just when they do great things — will bolster their self worth even when they're not feeling good about themselves.

Praise for their effort, for example: "you are getting better and better at these spelling tests" or "I am proud of you for practicing dance every day." With this kind of praise, kids put more efforts into things. They are motivated by your practice and hard work towards goals.

Set goals.

Articulating goals, large and small, and achieving them makes kids feel strong. Help your child turn desires and dreams into actionable goals by encouraging them to make a list of things they'd like to accomplish. Then, practice breaking down long-term goals into realistic benchmarks. You'll be validating their interests and helping them learn the skills they'll need to attain their goals throughout life.

Excite your children about their goals and ambitions. Show that you are excited for them, too. The positive energy and adrenaline will push them to continue their hard work and be happy with their efforts.

Celebrate Accomplishments When your child accomplishes their goals, let them know that you are proud of them. Celebrate these things together. In some cases, reward your child for their hard work.

Catch kids doing something right.

You arranged the dining table without being asked- That's terrific.

I was watching you doing your project work very sincerely.

These statements will do more to encourage good behaviour over the long run.

Your love, hugs, and compliments can work wonders. Ultimately, you are able to grow more of the behavior you would like to see.

A motivated individual has defined directions in life, and they know how to go about achieving life goals.

As parents, you can develop these qualities in your kids easily while being at home.

Tasks	Monday	Tuesday	Wednesday	Thursday	Friday	Saturday	Sunday
For example: Completed my Homework							

Reward Chart: Yes! You can do it, ____________________ (Child's name)

Appreciate them and attach rewards to their performance and achievements to motivate them.

MORAL OF THE CHAPTER:

✓ As a parent, our words become the internal language in the minds of our children. We know that our kids are capable of so much—let your words match this belief.

✓ Words of encouragement for kids can be the spark that helps your children develop a growth mindset.

✓ Acknowledge every effort of your child.

✓ Celebrate a little accomplishment of your child.

✓ Fill the reward chart given in this chapter.

3

HOW TO DEAL WITH THE BEHAVIORAL ISSUES OF CHILD

"The sign of great parenting: is not the child's behavior
The sign of truly great parenting is the parent's behavior."

‣ Why they lie and what parent should do

We know kids might lie because of the fear, fear of punishment, fear of anger, or to avoid trouble. Children may lie because of higher expectation of parents. There may be many other reasons why they lie but what is important is how to handle this. How to overcome this and how to encourage them to tell the truth.

• Your child may lie because they feel a lot of pressure to act in a certain way.

First assure them that you are as a parent there with them in any situation. Convince them, that your love is unconditional. You love them whether their grade in school is up to the mark or not. Convince them that you love and support them always in any adverse condition.

• Your child may lie because they are stressed.

As a parent you can analyze your child's body language, you can analyze that something happened and your child is hesitating to say. So tell them not to hesitate, I am there for you always. Be supportive, encourage them to tell the truth, hug them, help to boost their confidence, and when your child says something that is unexpected by you, just say it's ok, no problem. For example, if they say that their result is not up to the mark or their teacher scolded them. Your answer will be "no problem". We will try our best next time. Here your answer is we will try means you will support your child so that most of your child's stress is gone. They feel protected. They feel stronger with your support and this behavior impacts a lot on your child. Ultimately you are leading them to tell the truth.

Most of the time reason for lie is low self esteem of your child as well as higher expectation of you from your child. If you are able to create trust worthy environment surrounding them they will definitely tell you the truth. It will raise your child's self esteem and as a result they will be able to fulfill your expectation too.

• **Appreciate them for their honesty.**

Appreciate them when they tell you the truth. If they have done something wrong and they admit to you, appreciate them at that particular moment. Praise their dare to say truth. It will create a protective atmosphere for them. They feel stress free and as a result they are able to say truth to you whenever they have made some mistake. Tell them let's work together to sort things out.

Whatever the mistake is done by them never be harsh to them never punish them, instead, focus on solution. Sit with them to try and resolve the problem with them. Be supportive. You can also do this by emphasizing the importance of honesty in your family and helping children understand what can happen if they lie.

Talk to your child about the natural consequence of lying. Explain that dishonesty will make it hard for you to believe them next time, even if they're telling the truth.

Admit your mistake too in front of your child, be role model for your child. Tell them that we all are human beings and it's natural to make mistakes only important is that try, don't let it happen again.

▸ How to deal with stubborn child

One of the main reasons of child stubbornness is reinforce negative behavior by parents only.

They may become defiant if they feel that they aren't being heard. Most of the time, when your child insists on doing or not doing something, listening to them and having an open conversation about what's bothering them can do the trick. For example, if your child is throwing a tantrum to finish lunch, then do not force-feed your child. Instead, ask them why they do not want to eat and listen – it could be because they are playful or having a tummy ache.

If you want your stubborn five-year-old child to listen to you, try to approach calmly and practically and not head-on.

- ***Recognize yourself. (Never say no)***

How many times you say 'no' to your child in a day. The average toddler hears the word 'no' an astonishing 400 times a day, according to experts. That's not only tiresome for you but it can also be harmful to your child.

Saying 'no' again and again can become ineffective when it's overused. As a result some kids start to ignore your word. This may turn into stubbornness.

Your child asks you for ice cream while you're shopping. You say "No ice-creams before dinner." He stomps his feet. You say no again more sharply this time."Some children can't understand or learn the reason for the rule if they only hear the word no" , says Bruce Grellong, Ph.D., chief psychologist at the Jewish Board of Family and Children services in New York city. So next time try reframing your 'no' as a 'yes". For example, you could say to your child, "yes, you can have ice cream after dinner. Let's go look for an apple for now."

You can also use the ***art of distraction***. In this, if you are not willing to let your child to do a certain activity, you can divert their mind in other more interesting activity.

- **Explain your feelings.**

Consider explaining to your child why her behavior — such as banging on the table over and over again — is so bothersome to you. You might tell her, "You're hurting the table when you bang on it, and that makes me sad. Please stop." While it may feel futile to reason with a toddler, you're actually teaching her something: "You're showing your child that what she does affects other people around her — and you're giving her a crash course in empathy," says Leigh Thompson, a professor of dispute resolution at Northwestern University's Kellogg School of Management and a mother of three. "It may take a while for your kid to develop concern for others' feelings, but reminding her of your perspective will help her along," she says.

- **Give him/her a choice**

Your preschooler is throwing his ball in the living room, and you're bracing yourself for the sound of something crashing. Instead of saying, "No! No balls indoors," try saying, "You can roll the ball indoors or take it outside and throw it — your choice." Why? By offering him an option, you help your child feel like he has some power over the situation. "For kids between the ages of 1 and 3, this also encourages them to make simple choices and develop a sense of independence and competence,"

• **Discipline your child**

However, children also need some rules and discipline. Your child should know that there will be consequences, good or bad for their actions.

Make sure that they are fully aware of the consequences of breaking the rules.

Consequences should be immediate, especially when you are dealing with children so that they can connect their actions to the result. Time-outs, cutting down playtime, or TV time and assigning little chores can be a few ways to discipline the child. You could also get creative with consequences, based on the problem.

Remember that the idea is not to punish the child but make them realize that their behavior is wrong.

Stubbornness in children is common, but dealing with it daily may be exhausting for parents. However, knowing some tips on how to deal with a stubborn child could be helpful. While you must remain calm, listen to your child, and respect their opinions. However, do not give in to their demands or them; you might try giving them options and negotiating with them. You may also discipline them, but keep in mind that the goal is not to punish the child but to make them know that their conduct is inappropriate.

• **Offer a short explanation.**

Giving a short explanation about why you are saying no, can turn your refusal into a learning experience. "No! You can't go outside for playing", without an explanation your child may think "I cannot do that because my mom is mean."

Instead, try saying something like, "no you can't go outside because it is too hot, you can go for playing in the evening. I will also join you." In this way, your child understands the reason behind your refusal, as well as, when you say that you will accompany your child, he/she will be more happy. It is important that you grant permission to your child to do the activities that are good for their development.

▸ *How to deal with hyperactive child*

In present time one of the most common problems with children is that, they are hyperactive.

There are number of behavior that can indicate hyperactivity in your child such as:

- Inability to focus on one activity.
- Problems following instructions and processing information.
- Having an inability to sit still for calm activities like eating and having books read to them.
- Constantly being in motion.
- They are impulsive, overenthusiastic and bouncing with energy.

Hyperactivity is related to the brain. Hence, the best way to handle hyperactive kids is to make them relax and take things one at a time.

So, help your child to pay attention, focus better, and be less hyper.

• ***Channelize child energy***

In order to utilize their energy and calm their mind children need to be involved in out door activities and play a lot.

Engage them in classes that help them use up their energy, physical activity, and soothe the mind.

You can also involve them in brain game like puzzle, Sudoku or memory game. This will help boost their memory skills and concentration too.

Your child may do well if they're allowed to burn off excess energy through playtime before they're expected to sit still for a number of minutes.

If you encourage your child to utilize their energy in proper manner, they can do anything. For example, ***ROBIN WILLIAMS was one of America's best-loved comedian-actors. His hyperactivity, resulting from ADHD, worked to his advantage leading to parts in 27 movies during the 1990s alone. Mrs. Doubtfire and Jumanji are a couple of his major hits.***

Music to Calm the Mind

Music is a great way to unwind after school. Music exercises both sides of the brain at the same time, thus calming the brain, which in turn makes your kids multi-task and store information better.

When they are part of a band, or sing chorus, they learn also to be a team player.

- ***Take them in the lap of nature***

Nature has its own ways to soothe a hyperactive child.

And trust me, kids will love to be in natural surroundings.

Trekking, hiking, rock-climbing, rowing, etc. are great options for your bundle of high-energy.

- ***Engage them in mind games***

Games like scrabble, chess, matching pairs, etc. are great exercises for the brain.

These are engaging options for hyperactive kids as they make them sit in one place and concentrate.

• ***Utilize Positive Reinforcement***

Task completion is a huge struggle for a hyperactive child. Therefore, it is important that the child realize that the task is worth completing. Give praise and rewards whenever the child successfully completes a task. Rewards can be kind words, a hug, a chocolate, or a fun activity later on. This process empowers your child to associate extended periods of desired activity levels with positives.

• ***Practice relaxation techniques with child***

Learning about, practicing, and teaching your child about relaxation techniques may help to increase their awareness and understanding of their bodies, feelings, behavior, and hyperactivity.

These can include deep breathing exercises, simple stretching exercises of muscles, meditation, visualization, and yoga. There are more relaxation techniques out there as well!

Keep trying to implement new techniques until you get desired result.

‣ *How to deal Child Anger*

Learning to manage angry children and teens is an ongoing process and an important skill to learn.

As a parent first you have to discover the reason for the anger of your child. Here I am trying to give some more clarity regarding this. There may be some underlying medical conditions because of which your child may get angry.

ADHD: In this condition child may find it very hard to comply with instructions or switch from one activity to another and that makes them appear defiant and angry.

Anxiety: when your child feels fearful, stressed and finds difficulty in completing any task, it may create anxiety. As a result, they may outburst.

However, there are multiple factors which can contribute to a particular child's struggles with anger, irritability, and aggression (behavior that can cause harm to oneself or another). One common trigger is frustration when a child cannot get what he or she wants or is asked to do something that he or she might not feel like doing.

Environment is a contributor as well. Trauma, family dysfunction and certain parenting styles (such as harsh and inconsistent punishment) also make it more likely that a child will exhibit anger and/or aggression that interfere with his or her daily life.

• ***Stay calm***

Many times parents deal with angry outbursts by challenging their kids and yelling back. But this will just increase your feeling of being out of control. The best thing you can do is remain calm in a crisis.

If you come back at them with an aggressive response,

And say, "What are you talking about, that was your fault," the tension just stays at that heightened place.

So don't challenge your child when he's angry. That's just adding fuel to the fire. Instead, patiently wait until he calms down.

Remember, you're lending your children your strength in these moments. By staying calm, you're showing them how to handle anger. By staying calm, you're not challenging your child to engage in a power struggle.

When you don't respond calmly, your child will work even harder at his tantrum to try to get you to pay attention to him. So you have to tap into some solid parenting skills to handle the outburst quickly and effectively.

• ***Anger Management Skills***

One of the best ways to help a child who feels angry is to teach them specific anger management techniques. Taking deep breaths, for example, can calm your child's mind and their body when they are upset. Going for a quick walk in the garden , reverse counting from 100 or just engage them in their hobby like painting, art and craft or any outdoor game will be definitely helpful to calm your child.

Physical activity helps to reduce stress so encourage your child to do some enjoyable physical activities.

You can also develop a habit in your child to use some calming word or phrases repeatedly when they are irritated or not feeling good for example

"All is well", "Take it easy".

Criticizing or placing blame might only increase tension. Instead, use "I" statements to describe the problem. Be respectful and specific. For example, say, "I'm upset that you have messed up your room “instead of saying that "You never keep your room tidy."

• ***Don't Give In to Tantrums***

Sometimes kids discover that angry outbursts are an effective way to get their needs met. If a child throws a temper tantrum and their parents give them a toy to keep them quiet, they will learn that temper tantrums are effective.

If you change your mind after the child has gotten angry, you will be rewarding the behavior and making it more likely that they will try to manipulate you again the next time you say no

Don’t give in to your child to avoid a meltdown. Although that may be easier in the short-term, in the long run giving in will only make behavior problems and aggression worse. Instead, work on connecting with your child so they feel more confident that their needs will be met.

Consistent discipline is necessary to help your child learn that aggression or disrespectful behavior isn't acceptable. If your child breaks the rules, follow through with a consequence each time. For example If your child breaks something when they are angry, have them help repair it or do chores to raise money for repairs.

- ***Avoid Violent Media***

Research by psychologists L. Rowell Huesmann, Leonard Eron, and others starting in the 1980s found that children who watched many hours of violence on television when they were in elementary school tended to show higher levels of aggressive behavior when they became teenagers.

The resulting report and a follow-up report in 1982 by the National Institute of Mental Health identified these major effects of seeing violence on television:

Children may become less sensitive to the pain and suffering of others.

Children may be more fearful of the world around them.

Children may be more likely to behave in aggressive or harmful ways toward others

If your child displays aggressive behavior, exposing them to violent TV shows or video games may exacerbate the problem. Focus on exposing them to books, games, and shows that model healthy conflict resolution skills.

• ***Discipline your child instead of punishment***

Don't Get Physical with Your Child. Remember, if you get physical with your child, among other things, you're just teaching him to solve his problems with aggression.

Often parents forget that the point of disciplining children is to give them firm guidelines and limits so that they do not need to be punished. Disciplining means setting up boundaries and expectations so that kids know what is anticipated of them. The primary goal is to have kids learn to eventually regulate themselves so that they do not need to be punished.

Approach things from a more positive perspective by talking about what can be done better. If your child is whining or talking back to you, show them some examples of how to speak in a nice and friendlier manner.

After tempers have cooled on both sides, try a light-hearted game of speaking nicely to each other to express you better. If your child is fighting with a sibling, suggest some ways they can build a good sibling relationship, such as by having them work together on a project.

Behavior Chart (Child name) _________

1	2	3	4	5	6
7	8	9	10	11	12
13	14	15	16	17	18
19	20	21	22	23	24
25	26	27	28	29	30

This is a monthly behavioral chart

You can give a star or emoji to your children according to their behavior. When they collect 10 stars, give them a small gift for more appreciation.

MORAL OF THE CHAPTER:

✓ One way to encourage good behavior is to use a reward system.

✓ Being consistent is important because rewarding and punishing the same behavior at different times confuses your child.

✓ Try to understand your child's feeling and explain your feelings too.

✓ Avoid violent videos on the screen.

✓ Work with patience.

✓ Use the given behavioral chart to reward their good behavior.

4

EFFECTIVE WAYS TO STRENGTHEN THE PARENT-CHILD BONDING

Children don't say,
"I had a hard day, can we talk?"
They say,
"Will you play with me?"

Forming a connection with your child is important to developing a strong parent-child relationship.

The Parent-Child Relationship is one that nurtures the physical, emotional and social development of the child. It is a unique bond that every child and parent will can enjoy and nurture. This relationship lays the foundation for the child's personality, life choices and overall behavior. It can also affect the strength of their social, physical, mental and emotional health.

▸ ***Benefits of parent-child strong bonding:***

- A child who has a secure relationship with parent learns to regulate emotions under stress and in difficult situations.
- Healthy parent involvement and intervention in the child's day-to-day life lay the foundation for better social and academic skills.
- It helps the child exhibit optimistic and confident social behaviours.
- Promotes the child's mental, linguistic and emotional development.

- Children also gain strong problem-solving skills when they have a positive relationship with their parents.

How to strengthen the parent-child relationship

▸ *Be friend not parent*

When child is younger, they need to be parented but as they grow older they need you as a friend too. Perform both the task parenting and friendship simultaneously.

Parenting is the process of teaching, guiding, and leading the child to know how to make wise choice, to be disciplined when he/she is not making a wise choice, to be shown how to love self and others, to make friends and to evolve into wise, clever young person. Parent-child bonding should be strong in order to continue with this process.

As a parent you are laying a foundation for a friendship as your child grows. A parent-child bond is one of the special ones in the world. You can do both things at the same time being your child's best friend and raising them well.

▸ *Be there for them*

Author William Martin once said, "You do not need to make your children into wonderful people. You just have to remind them that they are wonderful people. If you do this consistently from the day they are born, they will believe it easily."

Tell your child he/she means the world to you and give them opportunities to feel good about him.

Tell them that your world wouldn't be the same if they weren't in it.

Sometimes all that a child needs is someone to be there for them. They might be going through something they want to discuss with you. Give them the window of trust and instil their confidence that they can come and talk to you. In such a way slowly and gradually your child will start sharing more and more things with you.

▸ *Make time for your kids*

Try to spend more time with them. If you give less time to your child they feel ignored. You can cook something together, you can watch their favourite movie together, simply eat meals together. This will strengthen your bond with your child.

Young children can develop many skills through the power of play. Simply join your child to play. it will be helpful for developing your relationship with your child and for fun. it can help children's language skills, emotions, creativity and social skills as well.

If you have more than one child, try to make a point of spending individual time with each of them. Quality, one-on-one time with your child can strengthen the parent-child bond, builds up your child's self-esteem, and lets them know that they are special and valued. Some parents schedule in special "date nights" with their children to create that one-on-one opportunity (whether it's a walk around the neighbourhood, a trip to the playground, or just a movie at home – it's important to celebrate each child individually).

▸ ***Listen to your child***

It is the general assumption of many parents that their child should listen to them and not the other way around. However listening to your child is more essential and effective than you can ever think.

Research has it that listening to your child makes it more likely that they listen to you as well. This is on the simple principle that when child feel listened to or understood, they are more likely to listen attentively and try to understand what the parent is trying to convey. Ultimately your relationship with your child will become stronger.

So by patiently listening to them, actively engaging in conversation, and allowing them enough time to express themselves at their own pace, you create a haven for them to express themselves and to find their own voice which is a very important aspect later on in their lives as well.

It is very important for parents to be able to communicate openly and effectively with their children. Relationship between parents and their

Children are greatly improved when there is effective communication taking place.

As well as child develop good communication skills. It will benefit children for their entire lives. Children begin to form ideas and beliefs about themselves based on how their parents communicate with them. Children then begin to feel that they are heard and understood by their parents, which is a boost to self-esteem. As a result children are willing to do what parents told. They are more likely to live up to parent's expectations.

Children feel secure in their position in the family, and are thus more likely to be cooperative.

- ***Love unconditionally to your child***

When parents accept, love, and show affection to their children, even when they make mistakes or fall short of expectations, this is love unconditional. In other words, it is a form of

love with no strings attached. Therefore, parents love their children for who they are, no matter what.

Unconditional love for my child meaning

For me, it's sort of as if everything else in the world has melted away and the only thing strong enough to remain is the radiating reverberating unconditional love I feel for my child.

Of course you love your children but tell them every day, no matter what age they are. Even on difficult days let your child know you didn't like the behaviour but you love them unconditionally. A simple "I love you" can do a lot to strengthen a relationship

However, the study also found that parental warmth and affection protect children against the harmful biological impact of childhood stress. Moreover, affection reduced the risk of adult disease. Therefore, the impact of unconditional love on physical health is undeniable.

Be a warm in your expressions, give eye connect, smile and encourage interaction.

▸ ***Hug your child every day***

Research has shown that children thrive in environments where they are showered with love constantly – and this starts from as early as the day they are born.

A 20 second hug can help your kid grow smarter, healthier, happier, more resilient and closer to you.

Author and family therapist Virginia Satir once said, "We need four hugs a day for survival. We need eight hugs a day for maintenance. We need 12 hugs a day for growth". Indeed, the importance and benefits of hugging are boundless as it does wonders to a child's cognitive and emotional development, and you as parents should not worry about hugging your child excessively.

A young child needs a lot of different sensory stimulation for normal development. Skin contact, or physical touch such as hugging, is one of the most important stimulation required to grow a healthy brain and a strong body.

Studies show that hugging can instantly boost the level of oxytocin. When oxytocin is increased, several growth hormones, such as Insulin-like Growth Factor-I (IGF-1) and Nerve Growth Factor (NGF), are increased as well10. As a result, the nurturing touch of a hug enhances a child's growth.

Oxytocin increases one's willingness to reduce fear, accept risk and trust others to improve relationships. It also increases a child's attachment security, leading to secure attachment and improved parent-child bonding.

MORAL OF THE CHAPTER:

✓ Under the roof of a parent-child strong bonding, a child feels secure and safe.

✓ Playing with your child strengthens your relationship and encourages your child to explore, observe, experiment and solve problems.

✓ Strong parent-child bonding removes a child's stress.

✓ Love your child unconditionally.

✓ Listen to them.

✓ It helps to develop your child's genius self.

5

8 THINGS RESPONSIBLE PARENTS DON'T HAVE TO DO

"The greatest gift you can give your children are the roots of responsibility and the wings of independence."

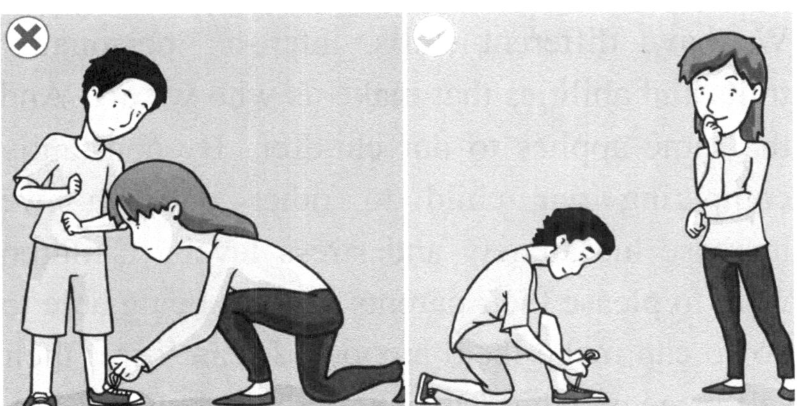

▸ ***Don't compare your child***

The problem arises when instead of observing our child's individual growth and progress and seeking help if needed, we compare our child to either his siblings or other children and judge him for being different. Why can't you read faster? Why can't you be neater? Look at Mrs. Shah's son. He studies everyday and gets 92 percent and above in all his subjects. We all fall into the comparison trap.

Theodore Roosevelt said, "Comparison is the thief of joy." By comparing our child to his siblings or other children, we run the risk of losing sight of what makes our child special and unique. All of us are different in our own way. We have different skills, interests, personality traits and abilities that make us who we are. And the same applies to our children. By constantly comparing our child to other children, we increase his anxiety and stress levels. Children want to please their parents and not being able to do so can make them anxious. It can lower their self-esteem when they start to believe that everybody is better than they are. They begin to feel incapable of being good at anything.

As a responsible parent, we can lay a strong foundation of self-worth and self-belief for them to fall back on. Keep reinforcing your message to your children. Teach them to take pride in their efforts and not just their achievements.

Never fall in the comparison trap to make your child feel inferior. Believe in the individuality of your kid and stay away from unnecessary comparisons and judgments.

Encourage them to be intrinsically motivated and not rely on external validation. And hopefully, we can raise our children to avoid 'the comparison trap'.

- ***Don't stop your child from voicing their opinion***

Children want their parents to listen to their point of view besides only speaking. Respect the child by at least listening to his or her argument/opinion, before jumping to a conclusion.

Children will like it if they realize that parents feel their opinion is important. It is not necessary for parents to agree with them all the time but they can at least listen to their child patiently. If you listen to your child they can express their feelings more clearly.

- ***It helps to develop the skill of decision making***

A key skill that children need to develop is decision-making skills.

Children who are listened are usually more confident then who are ignored. If parents give them freedom to voicing their opinion it will help to develop decision making skills of child.

Initially, children do sometimes end up making the wrong decisions, but they learn from their mistakes and try to take better decisions in the future. The skill develops further when they clearly understand the reasons for their decision coupled with experience and maturity.

Decisions taken by children affect their mental health and wellbeing. Their relationships and their success largely depend on decision making.

It helps children to become responsible and independent.

• ***It helps parents to connect with your child***

One of the important rules of being friends with your children is to treat them as equals. Give them an opportunity to place their opinion. Involve them in the decision-making process in the house. Be it about which new microwave to upgrade to or which place to visit during the weekend ask them for their opinion and why they think that Plan A is better than Plan B. Make them feel that it's important for you to know what they think and then go with their suggestions whenever you can.

Exploring opinions and ideas is one of the ways your child works out where they fit in the world. Your child's opinions might be different from yours, but taking them seriously sends the message that you value your child.

• ***It helps to make child independent***

Allowing our children to put their opinion gives them a sense of control and domain over their lives. Decisions also lead to independent thinking and independent actions and boost child's self-esteem.

Kids need practice for making choices and weighing pros and cons. plus, when making their own choices they take ownership of those choices. They learn from their bad decisions and cannot blame anyone else for them. Ultimately it will be helpful to raise an independent, successful, smart adult.

- ***Don't be over protective***

Wendy Mogel says that: Real protection means teaching children to manage risks on their own, not shielding them from every hazard.

Having protective parents is good for infant survival. It is also beneficial if the living experience contains high risks. But in an ordinary home free of serious conditions, focusing exclusively on protection without flexibility threatens children's development.

Parenting is an art of balancing and, in order to master it, you need to accept the fact you're only human, just like your child. Humans learn through observation and through real experiences: they make mistakes, they fail, they get hurt, and they become smarter in the process.

I know that for parents their children remain small always even when they grow up and they always try to protect them but to make your children independent let them handle their situation by their own. You can be there for them as a backbone and give them suggestion if required.

Instead of providing them with ready-to-use solutions, encourage your kids to come up with their own. This can be done through dialogue where parents take the position of mentors.

Many parents expose their children to stress as they seek validation from them. This creates a vicious circle: kids don't want to fail their parents while parents don't want to fail their kids. For overprotective parents, failing their kids means failing at raising perfect little geniuses or future presidents. They want their kids to reach their full potentials but they sometimes push too hard. For kids, failing means not living up to this standard.

Ultimately it will be harmful for their children's mental development as well as physical growth.

Though it is essential to ensure your kids are going in the right direction and are safe but being overprotective is what ruins the relation. Teach them about what is wrong and what is right, but let them decide for themselves. Give them enough space to choose what they want. In this way, they will not only trust you but will also be confident of their decisions.

- ***Don't force your child***

Your child would probably not accept authority if you force it onto him.

You should support your child's natural strengths and attributes to help them succeed where they are already engaged and passionate. By all means, encourage them to try new things and to step outside their comfort zone, but never try to force it as you will likely be met with resistance. Parents need to be clever and creative, understanding their personalities and be discipline. If you force your child to do a particular activity it will not continue the activity later in as they will always think as it was the thing my parents forced me to do. Parents should know that yelling, scolding or even repeatedly telling your child to perform a certain activity is not going make them do it. It has to come from the instinct, compassion and generosity.

It is important for parents to allow their children to decide what they want to become in future and how they are going to spend their life.

For example if you want your son to grow up to be doctor but he instead is interested in the arts. You'd like to see your daughter become a pilot but she wants to be a professor. What do you do? Make them follow your dream regardless of what they want to do? I know as a parent you worried about your child's future. Discuss your viewpoint and try to calmly convince them. But in the end, let them choose. Do not indulge your aspirations on your children. Remember, they will be happier that way and also be able to come to you with their problems in future. This will also prevent them from taking any extreme step if at all they fail to reach their goals.

Never force your child to be someone they are not. If your kid is shy embrace their shyness. Don't force them to be outgoing socialite and vice versa. Parents should also not force their children to do things they are not just good at. If your kid hates it and even after months of practice and training it is not learning then there is no point forcing your child to continue that activity? This will demoralize the child and deteriorate its confidence.

- ***Don't expect too much***

Most of the parents want their child to be the best in each and every activity, from academic to sports. Sometimes they become so harsh and start arguing that they leave no stone unturned to get their child the best facilities. So why shouldn't their children do the same to succeed?. Being under such intense pressure can have serious consequences for kids.

Despite your good intentions, expecting your child to become the next Einstein can crush their self-esteem and affect their social life.

Kou Murayama, who focuses on motivation and cognition as an associate professor of psychology at the University of Reading, in England, studied 3,530 German students in grades 5 to 10, and their parents, between 2002 and 2007. He and his team examined the results of annual math tests given to students. They also looked at a questionnaire portion of the tests, in which parents specified the grades they hoped their children would earn, and the grades they thought their children could reasonably earn.

While high parental aspirations led to increased academic achievement, that occurred only when parents' expectations were realistic, the researchers found. When their aspirations exceeded what their children could reasonably achieve, the adolescent's achievement declined, they found.

"Although parental aspiration is an important vehicle through which children's academic potential can be realized, excessive parental aspiration can be poisonous," Murayama wrote in the conclusion of his report.

▸ ***Harmful effects of parents' pressure***

• ***Damage self-esteem:*** Pushing kids to excel can damage their self-esteem. The constant stress to perform interferes with children's identity formation and causes them to feel like they're not good enough or even that they will never be good enough.

• ***Risk of Mental illness:*** Kids who feel like they're under constant pressure can experience constant anxiety. High amounts of stress can also place children at a greater risk of developing depression or other mental health conditions.

• ***Child may try to cheat:*** When the focus is on achievement rather than learning, kids are more likely to cheat. Whether it's a young child catching a glimpse of a classmate's answer on a test, or a college student paying someone to write a term paper, cheating is common among kids who feel pressure to perform well.

▸ ***Don't suppress curiosity of your child.***

During the journey of childhood children have lots and lots of questions. They just try to understand this world. They are curious about each and everything. Parents should answer their child which is very much helpful for their mental development.

Children want to know how things work, how things are related to each other, and what is safe and not safe. This world has so much to see, and they want to know how to explore our world. So, be patient and answer their questions. And, feel complimented that they are asking you!

Giving children the opportunity to be curious and explore their environment is important for their development and well-being. Curious children are more likely to learn and retain information, and stay involved and do better in school as well as in other activities.

Sometimes we suppress child's curiosity because we “don’t have time” or don’t have the ability to understand how important it is. If you suppress curiosity of your child then it is very wrong attitude. Children should be encouraged to ask questions and right answers should be given to them in simple words with examples. If the parents or teachers don't know the answer for a particular question or if they feel the children won't understand then also it should be communicated to them by using metaphors or if they don't know the answer themselves that should also be frankly confided to the children. If the children are suppressed, scolded or ridiculed for asking questions their self confidence will be adversely affected and serious behavioral problem would be developed by them which may continue through the life.

By allowing your children to be curious and explore, you teach them confidence and appreciation. You also show them the world and teach them the value of experiences over things. Explore with your children, get outdoors, and learn about the world around you. Curiosity will always open doors, and lead down new and exciting paths full of adventure and learning.

- ***Don't lecture your child***

Many parents spend enormous amounts of energy lecturing their kids about the importance of being responsible

To your child, it probably just sounds like nagging, and for good reason. It is nagging. And it's an ineffective parenting technique. Let me explain. Constant lecturing to your child gets in the way of his ability to be emotionally separate from you. You think your lectures are helpful, but they actually aid his irresponsibility.

I mean, it doesn't mean you interact less with kids. But if you find yourself you are a lecturing parent who has no set limit on the number of words you use while disciplining kids- pause and think.

Most of the time, parents start lecturing when children make the same mistakes again and again and children do not seem to get "why it is wrong".

And out of frustration, we may believe talking non-stop will help them to "realize their mistake and learn a lesson".

Studies show that lectures are not only boring but ineffective too. Children learn more by stimulating, active-learning methods

They don’t learn to be responsible if all you do is always nagging and pointing out their mistakes

They learn to tune you out and they don’t hear anything you are trying to teach them

Dr. Melanie Greenburg writes that “when parents go on and on, kids tune them out… The human brain can keep only four ‘chunks’ of information or unique ideas in short-term (active) memory at once. These amounts to about 30 seconds or one or two sentences of speaking”.

Allowing them to do so is a tremendous gift; even if they fail from time to time, failure is part of the learning process. Parents need to understand that it's okay to put their kids in charge, because it's only when they learn to practice monitoring their own behavior that they learn how to manage their own time and attention.

- ***Don't hesitate to apologize to your child***

Parents often have a hard time saying sorry, but it can be vital in showing your kids that you are human.

Some parents have been afraid that saying, "I'm sorry," makes them look weak or takes away their authority. On the contrary, it actually makes parents look strong. It shows that they care enough to take responsibility for their negative actions and make amends. Furthermore, children get the crucial message that their parents do not want to hurt their feelings—they are loved.

While you are the authority figure, you also need to show them that it is important to recognise when you are wrong. Everyone makes mistakes, and owning up to them is an important lesson.

• **Child learns to differentiate between right and wrong**

Understanding the difference between right and wrong is one of the most valuable lessons that your child will learn. As a parent, you help develop your child's conscience. By apologizing for something wrong, your child will begin to conceptualize right and wrong.

• ***Building strong relationships***

When you offer true apologies to your children, it will help build good relationships. Everyone makes mistakes. Acknowledging these mistakes is important in strengthening relationships. You will build trust with your kids, improve your bond, and validate their feelings.

Saying sorry to your kids is not a weakness. It is a strength to be able to admit your mistakes. You will show them how to apologize, why it is important, and that you respect them.

- ***Child learns to forgive***

Everyone makes mistakes, learning how to forgive is an essential life skill. Holding grudges can be harmful to both parties. By being able to forgive and let go, your children will be better able to navigate the world and their future relationships.

Cut out the shape of a heart from chart paper, scribble on it and give it to your child. Now, ask your child to clean the pencil marks on the heart using an eraser. Explain how important it is for him to erase any differences he has with his/her friends and forgive them.

Teach them that, by embracing forgiveness, you can also embrace peace, hope, gratitude and joy.

Consider how forgiveness can lead you down to the path of physical, emotional and spiritual well-being.

MORAL OF THE CHAPTER:

✓ Books contain information but knowledge is gleaned only through actions. The difference between warning your child about the danger and your little one actually facing it is a huge one. Being independent allows your child to start learning things by himself, take risks, and be better informed as a person.

✓ Encourage them, answer them always, let them take their own decision.

✓ Ask for forgiveness.

✓ Recognize your child's feelings.

6

TEACH VALUE OF RELATIONSHIP TO KIDS

"No significant
Learning occurs
Without a significant
Relationship."

Parents are the first teachers and kids role model. The way how we handle relationship forms the basis of their understanding.

This pandemic has converted the entire world into virtual living. That's the reason why most of the relationships are failing in the current generation. That means, we parents have to wear one more hat and teach the kids, the value of relationships and how to maintain them as human beings can't survive alone.

Human beings are a social animal that is why we like to live and move in groups. But in recent times, with the advancement of technology and gadgets, we are becoming gadget geeks and moving away from friends and families. People prefer the virtual world when compared to the real world and are happy living in separate life. In the gadget-driven world, the amount of time our kids are spending with peers and friends is getting limited and sporadic. This will automatically lead to the self-centered attitude in kids.

To avoid this, we as parents, need to provide more opportunities for kids to interact with people around him. The more he interacts with the people, the more he understands the importance of having friends and family around him.

▸ ***Show your strong relationship as a parent***

Children observe and learn from the parents about everything. So, they learn how much importance we are giving to our relationships with people around us and how we are maintaining them. Remember you are role model of your child. They follow you always.

In a study done by Robert Epstein and Shannon Fox, they reported 'relationship skills' as one the three most important 'parenting competencies.' According to the study, parents who show great relationships skills as a couple raise happier kids. Responsible parents behave like happy and connected couples to give good example to kids.

When you demonstrate that you accept your partner's quirks and habits (or tendency to make puns) instead of trying to get them to change, you show your kids that it's OK to be yourself without fear of being judged by others.

▸ ***Benefits of healthy relationship***

People who have healthy relationships are more likely to feel happier and satisfied with their lives. They are less likely to have physical and mental health problems.

Healthy relationships can:

- Increase your sense of worth and belonging and help you feel less alone.
- Gives you confidence.
- Supports you to try out new things and learn more about yourself.
- Lowers the stress.
- Research suggests that having social ties can increase longevity.

▸ ***Basic tips to understand the value of relationships***

▸ ***Teach them the importance of communication***

Good communication is an important part of all relationships and is an essential part of any healthy relationship. All relationships have ups and downs, but a healthy communication style can make it easier to deal with conflict and build a stronger and healthier relationship.

If we stop sharing our feelings with other people, that's when the relationship would start suffering. This concept could be taught to the kids even at a tender age when they keep fighting with their friends. Some kids shy away from talking after the fights with their friends. So, we need to identify that kind of kids and push them.

- ***Teach them to respect other's view***

Help your child to understand that, the more you listen, the more you learn about others' perspectives. Listening thoughtfully, without judgments or interruption, is also a show of caring and respect. With stronger relationships come deeper feelings of trust. Once you have the basis of an honest, trusting relationship, anything is possible — even tackling the most difficult problems and obstacles.

Many times we see that kids are not willing to listen other's opinion. Kids need to learn to respect all the people around them irrespective of age. Also, they need to give preference to other's views and emotions as well. So teaching this at a young age will have long-term benefits for the kids.

Encourage your child to be a good listener, and make sure you model that behavior by giving him your attention when he speaks to you. Listening is a sign of respect and is an important skill for school, as well as later in life. Teach your child to really listen to what someone else is saying and try to understand their point of view.

- ***Help your child develop empathy.***

Empathy is the foundation of compassion, which is the foundation of values. Children don't learn empathy by being told to feel it. The only way kids can learn empathy is by being treated empathically, and by watching you respond to others with compassion and kindness.

- ***Make your child ready for acceptance***

Every individual is different and unique. So accepting them as separate individuals with different tastes and needs is the first step of building any relationship. We shouldn't demean anybody based on their body, tastes, needs, and other physical attributes. If we follow this principle as parents, the kids will also practice it. This principle is very much needed in today's world. "No Body shaming to anyone"

Acceptance helps to keep relationship healthy, leads towards greater intimacy and care for each other. When you accept anyone with all their limits and habits, you are more willing to listen and understand each other's perspectives and suggestions. All of this means acceptance creates a healthier, happier and more positive environment for the every relationship.

- ***Never take relationship for granted***

Any relationship would start losing its steam when both the person start taking it for granted. We need to express our love, affection to the other person as and when the time needs or just as a habit. Once the kids see their parents expressing their love, affection, gratitude, and various other emotions to each other, the kids will start becoming more expressive in their relationships.

‣ *Sharing is Caring*

Another stepping stone for a good relationship is the sharing and caring we bring into that relationship. We need to share our emotions and care for other person's feelings, and then only we can maintain the balance in the relationship.

To share is to spread joy. Sharing is also a critical skill that comes in handy when kids play and learn with other kids. It sows the seeds of empathy and helps in building the social skills required for a well-adjusted adult.

"Love only grows by sharing. You can only have more for yourself by giving it away to others."— Brian Tracy

MORAL OF THE CHAPTER:

✓ Through relationships, children learn how to think, understand, communicate, behave, express emotions and develop social skills.

✓ It's vital to teach your child respect to be polite with everyone.

✓ Make your child understand the value of every relationship.

7

NURTURING HEALTHY KID WITH GOOD HABITS

"We first make our habits and then our habits make us."

In the previous chapter we focused on all parenting skills as well as child's mental development, However child's physical health is equally important for their overall growth.

▸ ***Basics for a child's physical health***

- Nutritious food
- Adequate exercise
- Healthy living environment

First let's learn about nutritional value and child eating habits. As a mother it's your responsibility for your child to nurturing a healthy attitude towards food.

Ideally, all food groups are represented in a child's diet. No need to cut out bread or pasta, or over emphasize veggies. It's all about balancing a variety of foods from wholesome, nutritious sources. Having meals and snacks at regular times may help kids better regulate their appetite and eating, while also building healthy eating habits.

- Start the day with a healthy breakfast. It

refuels the body and provides energy for the day.

- Let kids help plan and prepare 1 meal each week.
- Eat together as a family as often as possible.
- Take time eating, and chew slowly. Chew each bite about 32 times. It takes 20 minutes for the brain to tell the body that you are full.
- Eat more vegetables and fresh fruits. Aim for a total of 2 cups of fruit and 2,1/2 cups of vegetables each day.
- Eat more whole grains. Examples include oats, brown rice, and whole-wheat bread.
- Drink plenty of fluids. Choose water, low-fat or nonfat milk, and low-calorie beverages.
- Serve a variety of foods.
- Read nutrition labels for serving size. This information can help you select foods that fit your family's needs.
- Eat nutrients reach food. Vitamin C,

Vitamin A, zinc, and protein are top priorities for child proper growth.

- Avoid sugar, instead of it use jaggery or raw honey.

Local, raw honey is full of beneficial enzymes, antioxidants, and nutrients. Rich in antibacterial, antimicrobial, and anti fungal properties, this tasty medicinal is a powerful aid to strengthen your child's immune system,

Reward children when they finish food.

Image of food pyramid

From this food pyramid you can get more idea about food intake and which food is required in how much quantity.

- ***Importance of physical activities***

In recent years, it's no big secret that playtime has decreased tremendously. Instead of going out and playing, kids spend time in front of their digital screens. As a parent, you must encourage them to go out and engage in physical activities.

Due to pandemic children spend excessive time in front of screens, from TVs to Smartphone to tablets. It is very much important to make them aware of physical activities too. As physical activities are crucial for their mental as well as physical growth. Physical activity has significant health benefits for hearts, bodies, and minds.

Look at this Physical Activity Pyramid.

It is a visual guide that helps you to know what daily activities and sports you and your child both can do to have a healthy lifestyle, what activities to do on a daily basis, and which can have a weekly or less frequency. With the help of this pyramid you can plan your physical activities properly.

Benefits of physical activity for children

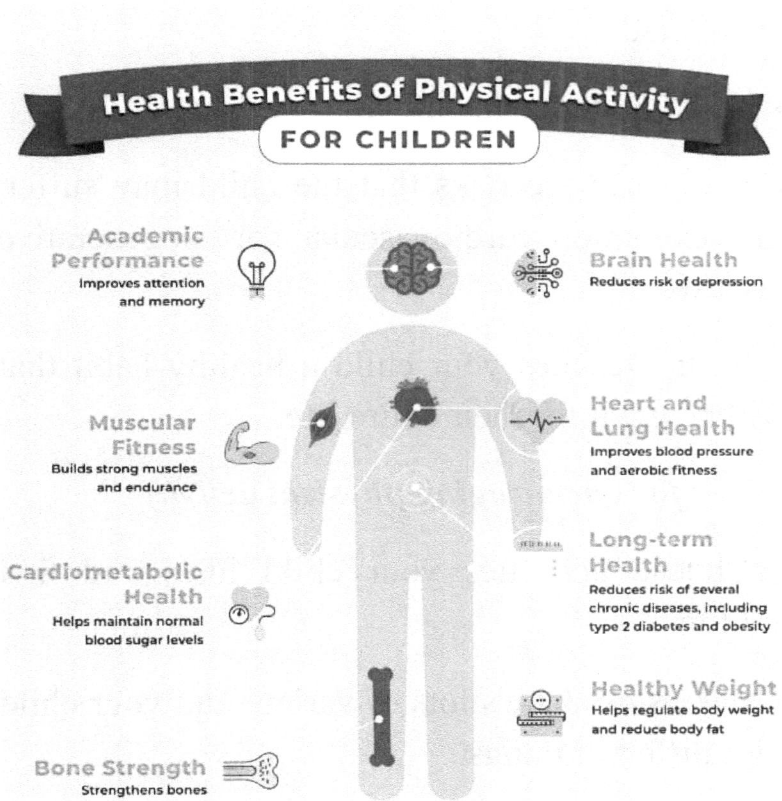

- It will develop healthy bones. muscles and joints

- It is achieved that the little one improves aspects such as coordination, strength, flexibility, and balance.

‣ It is also a way that children who do not know how to control their energy can have it "regulated".

‣ It will maintain healthy body weight.

‣ It reduces the risks that the child may suffer, for example, cardiovascular or degenerative diseases.

‣ It also teaches your child a healthy habit that will be great for their entire life.

‣ ***Tips for encouraging physical activity***

• Choose activities your child likes and that are fun.

• Make sure there's lots of variety and your child tries different things.

• Build physical activity into your child's day – for example, by walking to school, washing the car or helping in the garden.

• Reward your child with an activity like a visit to the park rather than with screen time.

• Praise and encourage your child.

• Be a role model for your children. Do something active every day.

• Be active yourself and involve the whole family.

Moreover, there are many other good habits which are helping to create healthy living environment for your child.

Having a good habit is like having a very important life skill. Just like clay, a child's habit can be molded easily when he/she is young.

Therefore, to make the future bright, parents always strive to ensure that their child learns and adopts only good habits and practices. Ultimately you can raise a happy, healthy, kind and successful human being.

Reading

▸ One of the most important habits for children to develop and value is reading.

It's important to note that successful people read. While they also read for pleasure, most use their reading habit as a means to gain knowledge or insight.

For anyone who needs inspiration about the value and importance of reading, look no further than the example of billionaire author, J.K. Rowling, who says she read "anything" as a child. She advises, "Read as much as you possibly can. My personal experience is that, nothing will help you as much as reading.

- ***Positive perspective***

According to many successful people, having a positive attitude is not just a result of being successful – it's one of the root causes of success.

Kids at this age get easily discouraged when things don't happen in their way. Teach them the importance of staying positive with healthy self-esteem and a positive mindset by telling them that they are lovable and unique. This skill helps them a lot in their life no matter what challenges they encounter.

It is not always easy to encourage your child to follow healthy habits. But do not give up as it is your responsibility! Try hard to make them learn because following these tips may help your kid follow a healthy lifestyle right from the childhood.

Developing a habit of reading good books is also helpful to develop positive perspective in life.

Teach them all the stories they feel excited about and make reading a part of your child's playtime and bedtime routines.

- ***Gratitude***

Foster a humble attitude in your children and teach them to be thankful for all things, big and small.

Teach your child to greet everyone with respect. They must be encouraged to regularly use words like please, thank you, sorry, and excuse me. The habit of using these golden words also makes one respected and admired in society. They must be taught how to communicate effectively with different people.

Teach them to be grateful for each and everything they have in present. Teach them to feel grateful before going to bed.

- ***Money management***

It helps them to learn the essence of financial responsibility and prevents impulse spending. Follow a system of giving them pocket money and asking them to make regular records of how they are spending the money.

It has been very rightly said that one of the greatest gifts you can give your child is handling money in a responsible manner. It will certainly follow through in his/her life.

- ***Teach Responsibility***

Every person is responsible for their actions. Children must be imbibed with this important habit for their own good.

One of the best ways to make them realize responsibility is by asking them to assist you in simple tasks like chores. Every family member has to do their part, and this includes the kids. Make sure they know that alongside playing with toys, there are other tasks to accomplish as well!

Praise your children for what he or she has done every time he or she displays signs of responsibility!

▸ *Value Time*

We must make children aware of the phrase "Time is money" and "Gone time never comes back". Children must be taught to make proper use of time and be punctual.

Make them understand the need of being on time to school, because they may be punished for not being punctual. As a family, you may attend several functions or parties. Make sure you reach before or on time for every occasion, and as the children grow, they will inculcate the same habit.

This time management skill is also helpful to them in future for goal setting and achieving.

▸ *Eat Healthy*

A good and healthy diet must be a habit. Children must be encouraged to eat fresh foods like fruits and avoid fatty and sugary snacks. You need to make them believe that even healthy food can taste equally good.

order to make children develop this healthy habit, go the colorful way – make it a target to eat each color of the rainbow once a week, which means eating foods of different colors in a meal. Not only does it has health benefits, but also ensures that the kids have fun eating.

- ***Enjoy meals together***

Make it a priority to enjoy dinner time together with all your family members. You can discuss a number of things and share your views with each other; this will have a long-lasting impact on your children. Other benefits of eating together include the following:

Children start getting comfortable and adjust well in the family.

Children develop good eating habits and avoid junk food when with elders.

Bonds get stronger.

- ***Maintain tidiness and hygiene***

Cleanliness must be taught to children by default early on in life. Start by organizing things properly around kids. When they get accustomed to seeing things in an orderly fashion, they will want to keep them that way too.

Teach them to wash their hands before and after meals or after playing in sand

Use clean dry towels, or maybe tissues, to dry hands

Brush daily and twice a day

Gargle post meals – This helps avoid bad breath and cavities

- ***Helping Others***

Raise your kids to have a helpful nature. Show them the path of humility and generosity. Encourage them to provide a helping hand to those in need whenever and wherever possible. Do your part; help people, be it a friend or a stranger, in presence of your kids, but at the same time, caution them to be careful with strangers.

Teach them that. Money is not only the way to help others. There are many other ways like, giving books, toys, food, sharing knowledge or simply helping anyone to cross the road.

- ***Teach child to focus on solution***

Children are excellent problem solvers and have many creative ideas for helpful solutions when adults provide opportunities for them to use their problem-solving skills.

Teach your child that, mistakes are wonderful opportunities to learn. One of my favorite memories from my childhood was my mom complaining about the dishes that were left in the sink. My brother quickly responded, “Are you looking for blame or are you looking for solutions?” Instead of focusing on blames focus on solutions. This skill is helpful to your child to build a successful carrier and live a happy life.

Good Habit Chart (child name)

____

Healthy habits

Healthy habits	*Monday*	*Tuesday*	*Wednesday*	*Thursday*	*Friday*	*Saturday*	*Sunday*
Eat Healthy							
Clean-liness							
Reading							
Exercise							
Value Time							
Home work							
Less screen time							

You can give a star or emoji, when your child finishes his/her task. You can even add other good habits as per your requirements.

MORAL OF THE CHAPTER:

✓ Healthy eating and physical activity don't become habits overnight. It takes time and effort to make them part of a daily routine

✓ Pay attention to child eating habits

✓ Monitor your kids physical activity

✓ Be a part of their activities to convert it into habits.

✓ Make them aware about other good habits.

✓ Ultimately it will be helpful to your child's mental

as well as physical growth.

✓ Use the food pyramid and physical activity pyramid given in this chapter.

8

KNOW YOUR CHILD BETTER WITH THE HELP OF PERSONALITY

"Attitude and personality are as important as experience and ability"

Parents, do you know why your daughter is so much talkative or why your son is shy?

Let me explain, because your son and daughter have different personality. We all have different personality. It can be a combination of genetics and how you were raised.

The concept of the four temperaments has been around since the days of the Greek physician Hippocrates (circa 400 BC).These he dubbed the four hummers: the Choleric, the Sanguine, the Phlegmatic, and the Melancholy.

Century later, ***Speaker Florence Littauer described the four temperaments with alliteration: Powerful, Popular, Peaceful, and Perfect.***

Here I will briefly describe about all four personality.

It will be definitely helpful to you if you can understand why your child behaves in a certain way. You can better understand why they are extrovert or introvert.

- ***Popular***

Outgoing, extrovert, storyteller, animated, spontaneous, good sense of humor, bubbly, loves people, makes friend easily, creative, colorful, talkative, exaggerating, loud mouth.

People with popular personality are playful and impulsive. They are constantly active and always optimistic. They have a good sense of humor, are entertaining, and are easily amused. They are also expressive and affectionate.

Famous Person with popular personality: Ranvir Singh

- ***Powerful***

Extrovert, adventurous strong willed, born leader, persuasive, competitive, confident, outspoken, bold, resourceful, motivates people action, organizes household, goal oriented, impatient, short tempered, bossy

People with powerful personality are extroverted and exude self-confidence. They are independent and strong-willed. They have quick minds and are generally active and practical in their activities. Their communication style is assertive and direct.

Famous Person with powerful personality: Virat Kohli

- ***Perfect***

Analytical, introvert, persistent, planner, scheduled, idealistic, talented and creative, sensitive to others, neat and tidy, thoughtful, serious and purposeful, genius intellect, perfectionist, high standard, hard to please, too sensitive

People with perfect personality are detail and quality-oriented, obsessing with understanding what is right. Also, they might be seen as paying strict attention to detail, which could make them out as perfectionists.

Famous Person with perfect personality: Warren Buffet

- ***Peaceful***

Introvert, controlled, reserved, patient, friendly, good sense of humor, good under pressure, hides emotions, relaxed, agreeable, not upset easily, inoffensive, diplomatic, good listener, unenthusiastic, uninvolved, hesitant, slow.

People with peaceful personality are service-oriented, exhibiting introverted personality traits, but will work with others to achieve a common goal.

Famous Person with peaceful personality: Sachin Tendulkar

All of us have different personality types. A person can have one dominant personality and other secondary personality. Person can have any combination of temperament types to make up their personality.

From the above explanation, you can better understand your child why they talkative or why they sensitive too much. You can help your child to overcome their personality's weakness. These descriptions also help you to recognize your quality. If we understand child's personality it will also helpful to you to decide which field or which activity is better for your child development and they can shine.

Always remember that whatever the personality of your child. Everyone can achieve success.

The belief must start with you first.

Believe first, and then take an action on learning and implementing those steps until your child reaches to the destination.

MORAL OF THE CHAPTER:

✓ The four different personality :

✓ Perfect

✓ Powerful

✓ Popular

✓ Peaceful

✓ This personality awareness helps you to know your child better.

✓ It helps you to know their comfort zone and decide a better career.

9

HOW TO DISCOVER YOUR CHILD'S TRUE POTENTIAL

"Every child born
with genius potential.
but giving every child
a chance to reach their full potential
is the best work a parent can do."

To prepare your children's success in the future, we need to get to know their talents and capabilities since early stage.

Every child possesses distinct set of potentials. While some excel academically, others choose sports, arts, music, etc. to make the most of their abilities. Children, from a very early age, start displaying the signs of their potential in the form of interests, habits and passion.

If parents keep a keen eye they can easily recognize where the heart of their child belongs to. The sooner they realize their child's abilities, the more time and opportunities their child will get to nurture their inner talent.

- ***Pay attention to your children's habits and hobbies***

Every day, pay attention what your children usually do and things they love. Their daily habits and hobbies can be 'something' to be developed further. Children love to do so many things. From playing to painting, or reading to running, there are a number of things they love to do through the day. And among these, there must be one thing that would interest them the most. Since your child spends the most time at home, figuring this out should not be a problem.

Your child's hobby might be the area where her/his real potential actually lies. Summer camps or weekend classes can be a great way to nurture your child's hobby and know whether they can make a career out of it. Talk to them about it to understand how far they are ready to take it.

- ***Notice your child in academic field***

Pay attention as which subject your child loves the most. Whether it is Mathematics, English or Science. They always focus more on the subject in which they are interested. You can also notice their keen interest by the help of their grades in school.

They are curious to know more about the subject which he/she loves. For example, if your child is better in Mathematics he/she can be good financial planner or chartered accountant. If he/she is interested more in science then you may help them to choose carrier as a data scientist or astrophysicist.

- ***Let them explore other activities***

Let your child try many positive things to dig their hidden talents. Do not limit to the academic field only. You can watch them doing their things, and when you spot new things that they love, you can guide them to develop other potential talents.

There's more to potential than just books and studies. Sports is one field which children are the most passionate about. The sport your child plays in his/her school can be the place where their hidden talent lies. If your child is passionate about any field other than education never hesitate to provide them with the professional guidance they need to excel in it.

- ***Study their behavior***

Notice their behavior how they communicate to their friends and other relatives. Watch them, how they carry themselves in their friend groups, family circles and social gatherings. How they treat others and represent themselves in the company of others, tell a lot about their personality and interpersonal skills. Children who know how to handle a situation all by themselves and have the ability to mingle around do really well in media, communication, marketing, sales, journalism or management. If your child's interpersonal skills are better than others and they like to take the lead, they will do really well in one of these professions.

- ***Importance of multidimensional field***

As parents we know that today's generation is extraordinary and extremely talented. They can nurture more than one field together. In present time competition is increasing so rapidly, that you can't guess sometimes which career is best after 10 years. If you look at some great leaders or check at the most interesting people in the market you may notice that they have one thing in common: they are "multidimensional" or at least extremely "curious" guys. You can also encourage your child to choose more than one fields as carriers. ***"Never leave any page unturned"*** For example, if your child is good in study as well as in extracurricular activities both together you can help them to choose academic career and excel them in other activities too.

Sometimes you notice that your child's interest is changed after some time. As they become more familiar with different things, their interests develop and also changes with time. As a parent it is your duty to recognize the field in which he/she can excel.

Most successful people have one thing in common; they discover their passions early in life and pursued them. This they could achieve only with the support of their parents.

A healthy family environment plays a very vital role in nurturing their potential to the fullest. The more inspiration they get from their parents to pursue a specific thing, the more motivated and confident they feel in their abilities. Make sure that as a parent you provide them with every support and guidance they need from you. Soon, you will see them blossom and making the most of their potential.

MORAL OF THE CHAPTER:

✓ Children exhibit a lot of potential from an early age. Parents need to keenly observe their children and make a note of their abilities.

✓ Pay attention to their interests and hobbies.

✓ Observe which academic area they love.

✓ Provide them plenty of opportunities to explore.

✓ Encourage your child's creativity.

10

OUR SUCCESS JOURNEY AS PARENTS

"When a mother and a father sees their new baby they see a tiny bundle of joy, they see perfection, and they feel love like they have never experienced before"

Parenting is a combined process and efforts of mother and father. In this journey of parenting my husband Dr. Bimal Ramani always has been there with me and Kaavya. He is a success guru and inventor. His vast knowledge, guidance and support are stepping stones for me and Kaavya.

He is doing research on Human powers and he helps people to achieve success and peace in their life. He can make ordinary to extraordinary within short period of time with the help of his practical programs. He is Amazon bestselling author of many books especially on "How to be Superhuman"

My inspiration for this book writing is my daughter and my husband. Reading and writing is my hobby. I wrote few books before this book but I have poured my heart and soul in this book. I am a mother of 12 yours old angel. Her name is Kaavya. She is my life. She is my whole world.

Nothing else can produce the joy or broken heart that motherhood allows. Motherhood is a wonderful experience. It can't be expressed in words. But whatever I read whatever I learnt and whatever I experienced during this journey of motherhood I tried to make all the parents understand. As parents we want to give our children, each and everything they want, we want to excel them in every field. All parents desire happiness for their children through guiding them with love, time and effort to reach success. All of you will definitely succeed in this; just follow the steps given in this book. Always be ready to learn for better parenting not only from this book but from everywhere, from everyone. Life is a new lesson every day. Learn that lesson, focus on your betterment and it will definitely help you.

However I want to remind you that because of the cut-throat competition in present time, parents tend to forget the most important thing which needs to be provided to children which is ***LOVE***.

Some studies proved that lack of parental warmth and love can make children more stressed, since parents put too much pressure on them to succeed without balancing it with affection. This can create health risks for children. In 2010, researchers at Duke

University Medical School found that babies with very affectionate and attentive mothers grow up to be happier, more resilient, and less anxious adults.

I know as a parent you don't need any proof to love your child. ***Just love - love and love to your child.***

I still remember when my princess came in this world and her small eyes looked around, I still remember when my daughter started crawling, I still remember when my princess first time speak a word Maa, I still remember when she started walking, I still remember when she achieved medals and ran to hug me with happiness, I still remember a lot of things which can't be described in words. I realized that you might spend thousands of rupees to buy something for yourself but one smile from your baby will make you the happiest person on the earth. ***Motherhood is a great experience and divine experience on this earth.***

Motherhood is a special bond that you have with someone that no one can take away from you. The bond I feel towards my daughter - I know that, no matter what happens, she will always be the most important thing in my life.

One more thing I want to admit that after being a mother I started to know myself. I recognized myself as a complete new personality. I recognized that there are many inbuilt skills in me which I never knew before being a mother. I and my daughter explored this world together when my daughter learns something I also learn something new as a parent.

I want to tell you something more, that the moment you become a mother, you start respecting your mother even more. All the things she did for you now seem so huge. You start wondering if you can ever repay her for the sacrifices she made for you. I love you mummy. I respect you a lot and can't express my feelings in words.

I know as a parent you all can touch my feelings as well as yours. All the best to you all. As a mother and father if you want to share your feelings or want to share something betterment of child please feel free to contact me on my Instagram.

I will definitely cover it in my next book with your name.

- ***Here I want to give a short glimpse of my daughter's journey till now*.**

I still remember when my daughter was just 3 years old she always used to stand in front of the mirror and look herself and smile as well as she liked to walk like a model. As a parent we encouraged her and at just the age of 4 years she participated in her 1st modeling show. She likes photography and she likes to give pose as well as she is talkative too. We recognized that she didn't have camera fear too. We make her drama videos upload on you tube and at the age of just 4.5 years she started her career in television industry in balaji telefilms show "pyar ko ho jane do". Now she is 12 years old and at this little age she did lots of television shows and made us proud parents.

Kaavya is intelligent in studies as well as in other extracurricular activities. She is creative as well as creator. At the age of 9 years she did art and craft work shop in our society as a mentor.

Kaavya valued her time during pandemic as she focused to learn many things. She started her motivational you tube channel during lockdown and inspired many people. She taught Bollywood dance by online class during this pandemic.

At present when I am writing on parenting she is also writing a book on how to achieve 360* success.

There are a lots of achievements of Kaavya in this little age. I will not be able to write all of them. You can watch her intro video in her motivational channel and can have more ideas about her success journey.

My dear parents, just recognize your child's inner quality, encourage them, support them, motivate them, do whatever you can. Your child will perform excellent in each and every field.

Please feel free to do any inquiry about any query on my Instagram. (@ramani_parul)

Follow my Instagram and you can subscribe my YouTube channel as well as my daughter's you tube channel to learn new things in parenting every day. You can watch her success

journey and can understand how successful we are as a parent. We started to sow the seeds of success in our daughter before pregnancy. How can it be possible, I will explain you in my next book which is on "Garbh Sanskar". God bless all.

Thank you to all for reading my book. I hope it will be helpful to you.

Feel free to give your opinion and ask the questions regarding parenting on Face book, YouTube channel (Parul Ramani) as well as on my Instagram (ramani_parul).

Thank you.

HEMISONS FOUNDATION PROGRAMS

Parenting

Garbh Sanskar
Parenting workshop
Parent councelling
Child councelling
Important aspects of family
Tailor-made program as per need
Women empowerment
Women self-help
How to become an independent women
Successful relationship

Success

Key to success

How to achieve 360* success

Dream big dream

How to be successful in life

Health wealth and happiness

Students

Unleash the potential

Speed reading

Stress Relief and Time Management

Memory power

Concentration and creative skills

Easy step to qualify in any competitive exams

Special Programs

Neurolinguistic program

Photographic memory

Power of universal energy

How to be healthy without medicine

Nutrition and diet awareness

Tailor-made programs as per individual need

Acting

ABC of acting

Basic acting skills

How to perform monologue and short scene

Drama, act and performance

How to be camera friendly

Voice modulation techniques

A to z of acting

Gateway of the television industry

Contact Hemisons Foundation for workshops and seminars in schools, corporates and institutes.

Hemisons Foundation

Dr. Bimal Ramani

Dr. Parul Ramani

Mobile : 7900092429

Email : HemiSons4all@gmail.com

: parulramani@rediffmail.com

"Mission of our life is to help people to fulfill their mission of life "

UPCOMING BOOKS

Sanskar

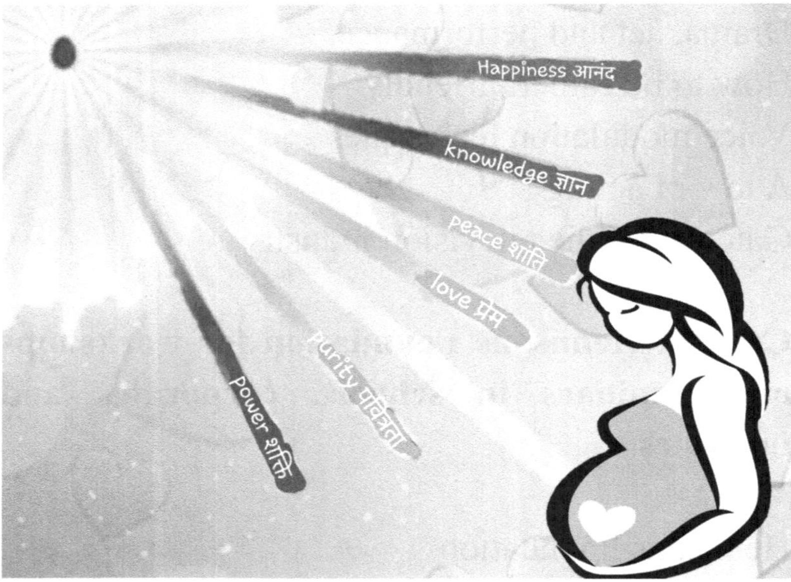

Successful Relationship